SEX AND THE CITY 2

THE STORIES. THE FASHION. THE ADVENTURE.

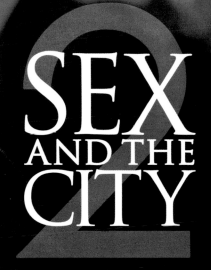

SEX
AND THE
CITY
2

THE STORIES. THE FASHION. THE ADVENTURE.

INTRODUCTIONS BY
Sarah Jessica Parker
Michael Patrick King

TEXT BY	PHOTOGRAPHS BY	DESIGNED BY
Eric Cyphers	Craig Blankenhorn	Number 17, NYC

PRODUCED BY
 MELCHER MEDIA

PUBLISHED BY
headline

 NEW LINE CINEMA
A Time Warner Company

 HBO

 VILLAGE ROADSHOW PICTURES

SEX AND THE CITY 2:
THE STORIES. THE FASHION. THE ADVENTURE.

First published in 2010 by Headline Publishing Group

1

Cataloguing in Publication Data is available from the British Library

ISBN 978 0 7553 6144 1

Printed and bound in China

HEADLINE PUBLISHING GROUP
An Hachette UK Company
338 Euston Road
London NW1 3BH.

www.headline.co.uk
www.hachette.co.uk

contents

from
sarah jessica parker

It seems our adventures never end, but I never imagined this one would take us so very far away from New York City. I was so glad it did, however, because after what proved to be an exotic, colorful, inspiring, difficult, incredible, unimaginable, and memorable seven weeks in Morocco, we got to come home. Having never worked out of the country with all four ladies together, and being so far away from our family and friends at home, we had the rare experience of not only working together, but of really living together, and I think we finished this movie closer than we have ever been.

We leave *Sex and the City 2* with memories of reuniting on fabled Fifth Avenue in New York City, riding camels, climbing the dunes of the Sahara, and navigating through the tiny corridors of the main souk in Marrakech. Recalling vividly all the foreign and wonderful sights, smells, and sounds that we would have happily stuffed in our luggage, and foods that were delicious, strange, and thrilling to try. The entire cast and crew eating breakfast and lunch under one big tent every day and watching the sun rise and set over our workplace. Being exhausted and driving back to our hotel past people and casbahs that reinforced how very far away from home we were and in what an exceptional time and place we found ourselves. The haunting and moving pitch of the call to prayer five times a day, singing show tunes, and planning what our first meal would be when we got home to New York City. And never knowing when we started the day what might lie ahead.

But mostly and most often, we were endlessly reminded of how lucky we were to be working together, and how fortunate we were to be having this once-in-a-lifetime opportunity. And to enjoy and savor every single waking moment. It was a unique and glorious journey, and I do so hope the experience of seeing the movie and browsing these pages allows you the same. Because, as always, we did it for you.

With love and appreciation,

XOX

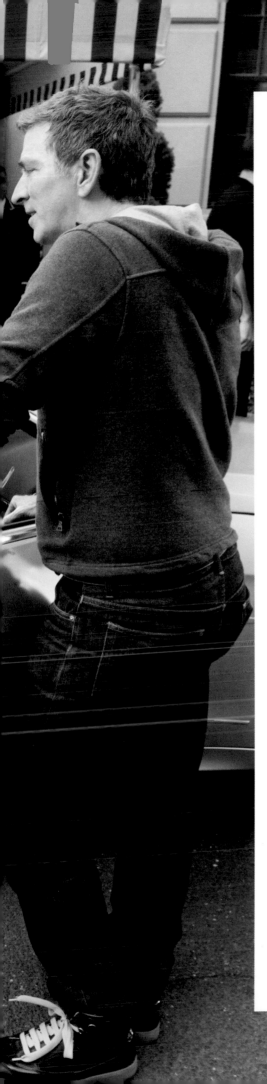

from
michael patrick king

Sex and the City has had quite a journey. What started out as a cable television series following the lives of four unknown single girls has evolved into a worldwide phenomenon—ninety-four episodes of television and two motion pictures following the lives of the now-famous female icons: Carrie, Miranda, Charlotte, and Samantha. As their characters matured, their worlds opened. In came careers, loves, heartbreaks, husbands, and, yes, even children.

So it seems only fitting that when I sat down to write the script for the *Sex and the City* sequel, the theme of "journey" came to mind. Not just the symbolic journey of the girls' evolution from past to present (as seen in the opening '80s flashback), but a literal journey as well. Being lucky enough to attend the first movie's premieres around the world and seeing the fans' excitement, I was struck by the fact that these four characters have friends around the globe. Why not let the sequel have a global feel?

This time I was more than aware of the downturn in the economic climate. There were reminders everywhere of how people were being forced to cut back and tighten their belts, and I thought—perhaps like the filmmakers during the Great Depression of the '30s did—that what might be in order for the sequel was a big, fun, decadent vacation for the girls on-screen as well as for the girls in the audience. And the immensely rich and stylish Middle Eastern cities of Dubai and Abu Dhabi seemed to be just the ticket.

I also chose the Middle East because off its deep roots in tradition—another major theme of this movie. I wanted to show how tradition not only affects the women in the Middle East, but more pointedly how we are still struggling with traditional roles even in a cosmopolitan city like New York.

So, off we went to film our big extravagant vacation. I hope you enjoy your Middle Eastern adventure with us. We had quite an adventure making it.

All my best,

Michael Patrick King

previously on
sex and the city

The first *Sex and the City* movie found each of our four favorite friends at a crossroads in her life. Carrie learned to write her own rules, Samantha struggled to regain her sense of self, Charlotte faced her fears, and Miranda allowed herself to forgive. No matter the challenges they faced, they handled them, as always, with their signature strength, humor, and style.

carrie bradshaw

After four blissful years together, Carrie Bradshaw and her "man-friend" Mr. Big finally decided—quite matter-of-factly—to tie the knot. But when a label-less dress was upstaged by a game-changing Vivienne Westwood gown, the wedding got bigger than Big—and Big got cold feet, leaving Carrie alone at the altar. After the big wedding that never happened, Carrie and the ladies went on the romantic "honeymoon that wasn't" at a beautiful Mexican resort.

Back in New York, Carrie got her unexpected single life back in order with the help of Louise from St. Louis. And when Carrie and Big finally moved past the mistakes they'd both made and remembered the love, they tied the knot for real—this time at city hall, with Carrie clad in a label-less dress.

Now Carrie is still happily married to the love of her life. They may have sold "Heaven on 5th," but they've found an even better apartment, one that is a little closer to Earth. For the past year and a half, Carrie's been transforming it into their beautiful home, all while finishing her fourth book, a funny look at marriage and the vows couples make. Now, as Carrie and Big enter a new chapter in their marriage, they're about to find out how serious those vows really are.

samantha jones

Samantha Jones always thought she was the star of her own life. But with hunky celebrity boyfriend Smith Jerrod, she decided to take a chance and be the woman behind the man for a change. Moving to Los Angeles and managing Smith's career made him a star, but it left Samantha feeling lost and alone. Thousands of miles from her three best girlfriends, she tried her best to make a new life as one half of a couple that lived in a gorgeous oceanfront beach house—where the ocean wasn't the best view. Tormented by her hot, oversexed neighbor, Dante, she turned to food to fill the void that her freedom once had. As hard as she tried to avoid him, she just ended up with a gut. Alone, naked, and covered in sushi, she realized that she'd found a loving man but lost herself in the process. So she left Smith, got a dog, and moved back to New York City.

Now the PR mogul is home—and at 52 and fabulous, she's back on the market in more ways than one. Thankfully Smith hasn't disappeared forever. He's about to help Samantha with a little business opportunity that will take all four ladies on the adventure of a lifetime.

charlotte
york-goldenblatt

Charlotte York-Goldenblatt finally got the family she'd always wanted. With husband Harry and adopted daughter Lily, Charlotte seemed to have it all, even though she'd always been told she could never have a child of her own. So when she finally became pregnant, it truly was a miracle. Yet Charlotte couldn't shake the feeling that she was due some bad luck—especially in light of the troubles her friends were suffering. Too worried something terrible would happen to the baby, she stopped doing the things she loved, until Carrie pointed out that you can't stop being who you are just because you're afraid. And so Charlotte regained her fearless self and eventually gave birth to a beautiful baby, Rose.

Whether organizing playdates at the Met or frosting dozens of ornate pink cupcakes for a birthday party, Charlotte is determined to be the perfect mother—the picture of style and poise. But with baby Rose entering her terrible twos, Charlotte's grace and patience are being put to the test by a fussy baby girl with a style of her own.

miranda hobbes

For Miranda Hobbes, balancing the duties of mother and full-time working lawyer was no easy task. And when you're that busy and tired, you forget to make time for the little things—like sex. So when Steve, her decent but ignored husband, made a "one-time slip" and cheated, Miranda was stunned. She moved out of their Brooklyn brownstone and back to Manhattan—the home of her former single self. Steve couldn't have felt worse and begged Miranda to forgive him, but she couldn't bring herself to do it. But eventually, with the combination of the reason in her mind and the feelings in her heart, she forgave Steve. They met in the middle of the Brooklyn Bridge and made the choice to move on—together.

Now that everything is happy at home, things aren't quite the same at the office. After years of hard work at her law firm, Miranda suddenly finds herself at odds with the chauvinistic new senior partner. Now the workaholic wife and mom wonders if it's really worthwhile to try to do it all.

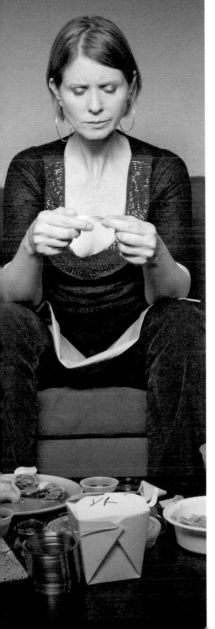

the making of
sex and the city 2

When the *Sex and the City* sequel became a reality, it was up to writer and director Michael Patrick King to create the next chapter in the continuing story of our favorite four ladies.

"I had the idea that this movie should be a party, and that since we're living in a financial depression, the girls should go someplace extravagant. All of a sudden Dubai popped into my mind, and then I thought how funny it would be to have these very opinionated, very sexually liberated American women in the Middle East.

"The theme of the movie is tradition and how you deal with that in your life, and I started to think more and more about how tradition would play in the Middle East. I knew what the main story points were going to be, but I didn't know the specifics. So the first thing to do was go to Dubai."

It turned out to be a great first date. "All of the doors flung open, and I had this extravagant experience. We flew on Air Emirates, which is the super first class airplane we duplicated exactly for the fictional airline in the movie. And the hotel picked me up in a white Rolls Royce and gave me my own butler, and of course it blew my mind."

King returned to the U.S. and wrote the script to mimic his experience in Dubai—from shopping in the souk marketplace to riding a camel on the red sand dunes.

THE COLORS AND TEXTURES DOCUMENTED IN MICHAEL PATRICK KING'S RESEARCH PHOTOS (TAKEN AT ATLANTIS, THE PALM HOTEL IN DUBAI) INSPIRED THE SETS EVENTUALLY CREATED FOR THE MOVIE

ON LOCATION IN MANHATTAN

MICHAEL PATRICK KING DIRECTS CYNTHIA NIXON AND SARAH JESSICA PARKER ON PERRY STREET IN THE WEST VILLAGE

KING, KRISTIN DAVIS, PARKER, AND PRODUCER JOHN MELFI SHOOT THE FLASHBACK SCENE ON FIFTH AVENUE AND 58TH STREET

After King finished the script and submitted it for approval, he began to scout locations with producer John Melfi. "We were in search of the Middle East, and we wound up in Morocco, where we had everything we needed and more," says King. "Morocco is a gorgeous, storied place, and they have a seventy-five-year history of filmmaking in that country. We had absolutely amazing experiences there—it couldn't have worked out better."

But months before the big journey to the Middle East, there was a whole lot of New York to film. In June 2009, the New York crew began casting, building sets, and scouting locations for the shoot.

Sex collided with the city and thousands of fans and onlookers outside the Plaza Hotel on September 1, 2009, when shooting began on the '80s flashback scenes. A film crew on the streets of New York will always draw a few curious people, but there's something about *Sex and the City* that people want to stop and connect with.

"Back when we did the series, I remember the beginning of the public awareness," says King of the early days. "One night, we were shooting Carrie and Aidan's big breakup scene around the fountain in Season Four. It was like 4 A.M., and a garbage truck came around the corner, and the guy hanging off the back said, 'Hey, Carrie, dump him!'"

The audience on set has grown considerably

22

KIM CATTRALL AND KING ON SET AT SAMANTHA'S TIMES SQUARE OFFICE

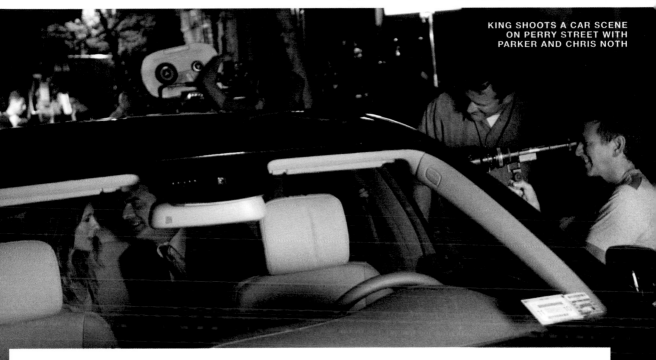

KING SHOOTS A CAR SCENE ON PERRY STREET WITH PARKER AND CHRIS NOTH

since then. Because a film permit only allows limited control of the city's crowds, anyone on the street can stop and watch the action—and they do, by the thousands.

"When we were filming the opening sequence with all four girls in front of Bergdorf Goodman—and I am not exaggerating—a thousand people were watching. We had a similar experience on the first movie. People feel like these four characters are theirs and they're part of New York," says King. "For a tourist, it's as if you went to Africa and saw a giraffe in the wild. You would be like, 'I just got a picture of a giraffe on the plains of Africa!'"

"It can get pretty crazy with the onlookers," says Melfi. "We have about forty production assistants locking up every corner; they get everyone to quiet down and not take any flash photographs, because flashes end up on film. It's really great how people cooperate." Adds King, "People sometimes ask me, 'Isn't it annoying to have thousands of people watching?' And I say, 'Wouldn't it be worse if no one cared?'"

Fans and the curious aren't the only ones snapping photos. On a typical shoot day, dozens of unapologetic paparazzi, with their trademark telephoto lenses, also flood the streets. "Because *Sex and the City* has such a long history, the paparazzi know the cast and the assistant directors, so they cooperate," says Melfi.

At least the shooting process itself has become quite fluid. "People ask us, 'How long

do you rehearse each scene?' and I answer, 'Twelve years," says King. "The women have been playing these parts for a very long time, and they know their characters inside and out. We've reached the point where we can say something with a look, because we all know each other so well.

"These four characters have great heart and soul and strength and vulnerability, and they defy aging in the best way," he adds. "I loved them in their thirties, and I love them in their forties and fifties. For me, they will never stop being interesting, as long as they are dealing with relatable topics that women experience. They would be fascinating in their eighties!"

After thirty-three hectic days filming in New York, the cast and crew departed for Morocco. For the next seven weeks, they lived in close quarters as they traveled throughout the country, from Merzouga in the Sahara desert to the exotic city of Marrakech.

Finally, the last chapter of *Sex and the City* came to an end on January 16, 2010, after a seventy-two-day shoot back in New York.

So will there be another chapter? "It's so hard to think about the life of *Sex and the City* beyond where we are now, which is, please let us have produced a movie worth our audience's hopes," says Sarah Jessica Parker. "If it's the right thing to do by our audience, we will, because they've done right by us for a really long time."

FILMING A DESERT SCENE IN MERZOUGA,

OVERLOOKING THE MEDINA

SARAH JESSICA PARKER IN MARRAKECH'S MEDINA, OR OLD CITY

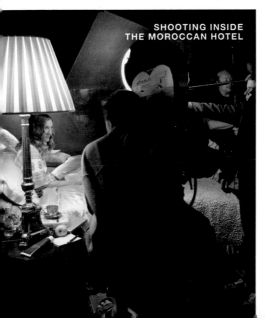

SHOOTING INSIDE THE MOROCCAN HOTEL

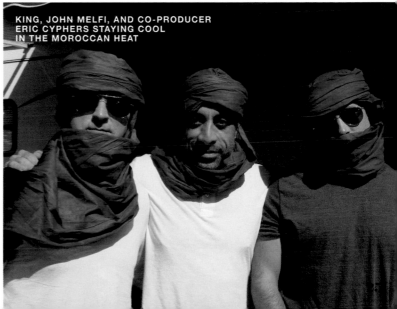

KING, JOHN MELFI, AND CO-PRODUCER ERIC CYPHERS STAYING COOL IN THE MOROCCAN HEAT

conversations
with the girls

Throughout the years, the lives of these four friends have taken them to new and unimaginable places—and so too have the lives of the actresses who play them. Relationships and families have grown and changed, and new challenges are always presenting themselves. Whether they're navigating the realities of dating life or coming to terms with the realities of motherhood, there's something universally relatable about each of these women—both on and off screen.

sarah jessica parker

*"This movie is really a romp—
it's big and very cinematic."*

ON THE SEQUEL

The first movie was really about how one deals with disappointment and friendship and love, and all the thoughts we have as grown-up people. This movie is really a romp—it's big and very cinematic, with big shots and massive production design. The costume design is intricate and involved. Shooting in Morocco—it just felt big. It was like we were doing our own version of *Star Wars*.

ON CARRIE AND HER CAREER

Carrie has spent her career writing about being single, and here, for the first time, she's writing about being married. The truth is, she doesn't know a lot about it because she's only been married for a short amount of time. She's not wearing it quite as comfortably as she wants to be. She's about to have her fourth book published. It's called *I Do, Do I?* Carrie is extremely worried about the reviews—it's a subject that she hasn't tackled with the same kind of comfort level she's had in the past, and she's feeling very nervous about the critical reception of the book.

ON FILMING IN MOROCCO

Morocco is breathtaking. It was so good to see such a beautiful people and country. To hear the call to prayer five times a day—I think I liked it more than anybody. It's one of the prettiest sounds, the competing voices of the mosques all around you. And when you're in it, it's the most beautiful environment you could imagine.

ON COSTUMES FOR THE MIDDLE EAST

We spent half of this movie in the Middle East, and that dictated a big part of the design, being in a part of the world that has certain religious, ideological, and therefore fashion requirements for women. It was a kind of math problem for us to solve, how to not be chaste and yet still be completely covered for a lot of the movie. There were occasions when we actually had to have our heads covered, so it was complicated.

ON SINGING KARAOKE WITH THE LADIES

Karaoke is one of the hardest things to do, but being with Kim and Cynthia and Kristin made it doable. I could never in a million years have done that alone. It was so funny hearing Cynthia describe her moves. She's like, 'This is one of my moves,' and she does a dance step, and you're like, 'Yeah, you could call that a move.' And then Kim's really bold and will do it for real. And Kristin is very demure, and of course ends up looking incredible in her kitten approach to it all. It was just hilarious.

ON AIDAN

It's a really pleasant reunion between Carrie and Aidan, and that's good given that the last time they were together it was pretty heartbreaking. Carrie broke Aidan's heart, and Aidan always loved her in the way that she had wanted to be loved. He was just the wrong person to love her that way.

ON MICHAEL PATRICK KING

I always say that for me, *Sex and the City* is like this family heirloom that somebody gave me and said, 'You have to take care of this until you are an old lady, and you'll have to decide while you're still coherent who it should be handed off to next.' And I think that Michael feels the same way. He protects *Sex and the City* that way and is fiercely vigilant about every detail.

I think we work really, really well together, and I can't imagine having spent this amount of time on something without him there to create the story. It all comes back to Michael Patrick and the written word. The clothes are wonderful and fun, but you hang your hat on a story, that emotional investment, and we don't have that without Michael.

kim cattrall

"Samantha speaks from a
tremendous amount of experience."

ON THE SEQUEL
The really exciting thing about the sequel is that it's only been a year and a half since you've last seen us. We're picking up exactly where we left off. This movie reminds me of the road pictures of Bob Hope and Bing Crosby, going off to exotic locations and crazy things happening to these quintessentially American characters.

ON THE FRIENDSHIP
Sex and the City has redefined family. Family used to be just what your biological DNA was or your boyfriend or your husband or your children. But this friendship is a family defined by choice and chemistry. I believe these four characters really do make up a present-day complete woman, and that's why they're so relatable.

ON SAMANTHA
There really is no BS about Samantha. She says it like it is. Being the oldest of the group, she speaks from a tremendous amount of experience in a healthy, positive way. I think there are few things that she fears or judges. Being sexual and knowing what she wants has been a very empowering thing for her, and I think for a lot of other women in the world: This is what I want. This is who I am. Samantha is a powerhouse and has integrated that philosophy into her life in a very healthy way.

ON 80S FASHION
I look at some of the things that I wore in the movie *Mannequin*, and I think, Oh, my God. You know, when you're young, you want to wear all that makeup, you want to be adult and sexy, and you work so hard at it. But as you get older, you relax a little bit and realize that less is more. But at that time, it was just part of being a girl, you know, dressing up and flashing it. It was fun.

ON WORKING IN MOROCCO
I've always wanted to go to Morocco—it has such mystique. In the Medina, the marketplace, behind these hidden doors are these amazing homes, *riads*, and they all have these tiny little doors that look the same. Sometimes you walk in, and it's quite poor, sometimes middle class. Then you walk through the same kind of door, and it's a palace. Everything is hidden and private.

It was so much fun riding on the camel in the Sahara with that leather headdress on, spreading my arms out with Sarah in front, feeling like we were flying. *Sex and the City* takes you to places you never thought that you'd go.

ON SINGING KARAOKE
We went into a recording studio, all four of us, and it was a dream to sit there. I felt like we were a girl band. We each had our part, and we all sang it completely differently, and then they put it all together. I mean, we're not professional singers, but we felt like we were for a day. To stand up on that stage and sing "I Am Woman, Hear Me Roar" was fantastic. We did it about two hundred times, but each time I loved it. It was like headlining in Vegas.

ON THE FUTURE OF SAMANTHA
I think that Samantha will continue to be this amazing force. I still don't see her in a settled relationship. And I think that's a very positive thing, because it's redefining what it means to be alone. I see Samantha happy. I don't see her searching for things. I don't see her hungry for something on the outside to make her complete. She's the right woman for herself. She's not going to compromise. And whatever happens, she will deal with it, with a tremendous amount of self-confidence and love.

kristin davis

"Charlotte is definitely more style conscious than I am."

ON THE SEQUEL

This is like a road movie mixed with a clash of cultures. We get to see how other women in the world are living, and also how there is a wonderful communal experience between women all over the world.

ON THE NEW WOMAN IN CHARLOTTE'S LIFE

When you see her, you will know why Charlotte is obsessed with her new nanny, Erin—she's quite gorgeous. Erin is played by a lovely actress named Alice Eve, a beautiful British girl. She's young and gorgeous and all kinds of clichés that you think about when you think about women who should not really be hired as nannies. But Charlotte doesn't see any of that because she desperately, desperately needs a wonderful nanny.

ON HER 80S FLASHBACK LOOK

For me, it was super easy because Charlotte was a preppy—not that far away from how Charlotte dresses now. I was a little relieved that I didn't have to wear some scary 80s wig.

ON THE DIFFERENCE BETWEEN KRISTIN AND CHARLOTTE

Charlotte's definitely more style conscious than I am. I surrendered a while ago to the idea that I was just going to let my fans down if they ran into me on the street. If I'm doing press, then I use a wonderful stylist, Elizabeth Stewart, and she tells me things that I'm not allowed to be seen in, ever. I try to do what she says, but I don't care that much. It's wonderful to get to play a character who cares a lot, but I don't put that kind of pressure on myself in real life.

Charlotte is not a Southern girl like me—she's from Connecticut, she went to Smith—but there are similarities between a New England preppy and a Southern preppy. Both care about being put together properly. I think those similarities have helped me with Charlotte. But in real life I'm much more rebellious than she is.

ON SHOOTING IN MOROCCO

I love Morocco, and Morocco is so, so, so different from the other countries I've visited. There's the really interesting mix of the European there—you're very aware that Europe is so close and the French have a history there. Morocco is like its own wonderful, very interesting mix of African and European.

The outfit I wore when we go camel riding was one of those outfits that was just, oh, a little crazy. But we were in the Sahara riding camels, so we had to push the envelope a little bit, right?

ON HER FIRST KARAOKE EXPERIENCE

I had never done karaoke in my life. I'm a shy singer, and Michael decided that we were all going to do that number in front of two hundred extras. We lived through it, and it was really fun, but we were so nervous. Singing karaoke was one of those crazy moments where you're just like, *Sex and the City* has a life of its own and we're just here for the ride, trying to hold on. It's like a bucking bronco, and we are just trying to stay on. The four of us rely on each other so much, and there's no way we would ever get through all of the things we've gotten through if we didn't. We're so lucky. I don't think it's very often that four women get to play such strong characters.

cynthia nixon

*"Miranda wants to enjoy things
and have fun and have adventures."*

ON THE SEQUEL

Miranda used to be so much more about winning and getting ahead, more diva-ish. But in this film she's sort of the cheerleader among the four women, taking emotional care of the other three.

ON FILMING IN MOROCCO

We had adventures, we went shopping, we ate dinner at each other's hotels, and we took trips. I won't say it was like summer camp, because it was far too exotic for that. But for our whole crew, it was a bonding experience.

Driving to work every morning for forty minutes—with no highway, just over the sand—was amazing, so beautiful and unspoiled. So many movies have been filmed there, like *Lawrence of Arabia*, so when you see it in person, you feel like you're in a movie, like you're on a set. It's like if you were to go see the Taj Mahal. You've seen it so many times, and it's so beautiful and so striking, but your eye almost sees it as if you were looking at it on a postcard.

I think Morocco is very, very different than Abu Dhabi would have been had we actually filmed there. Morocco is so used to foreign visitors and foreign residents, and has been for hundreds if not thousands of years. In a way, Morocco is like the Muslim version of New York.

ON MIRANDA'S EVOLUTION

Miranda was always smart. She was always tenacious. And she used to be so much more about getting ahead and winning. I think the combination of becoming a mother and having this very loving marriage made her begin to look more skeptically at her career and think, This isn't really all it's cracked up to be.

In the last film, Miranda got to such a strange place in her marriage—with her husband, with herself, with every aspect of her life. She was so tense, and so much of the enjoyment had gone out of her life. When we last saw Miranda and Steve, they were really at their all-time low. I think they've put in the hard work, and they've really gotten back to each other. When we pick up with her in this movie, Miranda wants to enjoy things and have fun and have adventures and not just be chained to a desk eighteen hours a day.

ON SINGING KARAOKE

When I think about the karaoke scene, I think about the day when the four of us went into a recording studio—even before we had started filming—and laid down the track. When we actually performed the scene, there were a few hundred people in the room. But somehow being in the studio with just a microphone was way more daunting—they play back the track and you can hear your voice. I'm not really a singer, but we did well—for us, we did well. You want to be entertaining and charming, but you want to keep in mind that in the movie it's a spontaneous thing, that the four of us get up and we haven't rehearsed, and maybe we don't know the lyrics all that well. You don't want it to be too choreographed because these characters aren't performers, they're a bunch of friends out on a holiday.

ON WORKING TOGETHER ALL THESE YEARS

We've known each other for so long now—it's been twelve years. My daughter turned thirteen during the filming of this movie, and she was eight months old when we did the pilot. It's amazing. I feel like we've all been through a lot separately and together. And we really love each other and support each other. We've spent an enormous amount of time together over these twelve years.

also starring

Sex and the City is a story about four friends who braved the dating world of New York City and not only survived but ended up with three good men. But where would they be without them?

"These women would be spinning in a false reality if the men in their lives weren't worthwhile. The guys are really important," says Michael Patrick King. "It's always been about the four friends. But their lives wouldn't have evolved in such a specific way if the audience wasn't somehow relating to the men that they chose."

the men

BIG

No man since *Sex and the City* debuted has loomed larger than the love of Carrie Bradshaw's life, the incomparable Mr. Big (played by Chris Noth). "There's a strong male point of view from Mr. Big in this movie. You really get to see him live this time," says Michael Patrick King. "In the series, he was in and out a little bit, and he represented something elusive. Now you get to see an interesting Tracy/Hepburn–male/female dynamic between Carrie and Mr. Big."

"People feel a connection to the relationship between Carrie and Big—it's romanticized but it's not. There's a lot that's real about it, and I think this pushes certain buttons for people who are in relationships, about their needs and wants for the perfect mate," says Chris Noth. "The reality is that a relationship just doesn't end with the wedding—you have a life together and all the ups and downs of that. So there's never a happily ever after per se. It's always a work in progress."

Says Sarah Jessica Parker: "It's a great privilege for me to know Chris. He's really let me in, and he counts on me, and I count on him. I think he really trusts me, and I completely trust him. I don't believe that anybody could have played Big but Chris Noth."

STEVE

Miranda and good-guy husband Steve Brady (played by David Eigenberg) have been down a long road since their falling out in the last movie. This time, Steve has Miranda's back, helping her through a difficult crossroads in her career. "I think that one thing that touches Miranda so much is Steve's support of her," says Cynthia Nixon.

"Steve was created specifically to soften Miranda," says King. "It was at a point in the series where Miranda was really sarcastic and opinionated and also really alone, and I thought we had to find an antidote to that. I wanted to introduce a guy who was casual and working class into this very glittery New York world."

HARRY

Charlotte is always striving to be the perfect mother with the perfect home, but she couldn't do it without her faithful husband, Harry Goldenblatt (played by Evan Handler). Harry, however, was probably the last man Charlotte could have imagined marrying when she began her quest for the perfect husband many years ago. "Charlotte's journey was always to find Prince Charming—a handsome, rich, WASP," says King. "And her great evolution as a character is that she was able to see past that ideal when she fell in love with Harry." Adds Kristin Davis, "I think it is so important that you see a relationship that's working. I'm so pleased that Harry has not let Charlotte down."

SMITH

Samantha and her sexy ex, Smith Jerrod (played by Jason Lewis), had a great five years together, and although he is no longer her mate, Smith is still in Samantha's life. "They've turned the page, but it doesn't mean that there is any animosity between them," says Kim Cattrall. "It was just time for Samantha to move on." The celebrity and his publicist may have moved on, but his career has only moved up. Two years later, Smith is now a big action movie star, his latest film is premiering in New York City, and there's only one woman he can imagine on his arm—even if it's just as friends. And it's there, at his film premiere, that Samantha meets a new man, one who makes her an offer that's too good to refuse.

STANFORD AND ANTHONY

Carrie's best gay friend Stanford Blatch (played by Willie Garson) and Charlotte's best gay friend Anthony Marantino (played by Mario Cantone) have each come to an unpredictable new point in their lives. But more unpredictable for Cantone was the cameo appearance of his real-life sisters, Marion and Camille. "My sister Camille doesn't leave Malden, Massachusetts," says Cantone. "She's too neurotic." But when the cameras began to roll, Mario saw a whole other side to her. "She was actually acting, and at one point I was like, Who is this? This is not my sister. It was my favorite memory—by far."

AIDAN

Before Carrie Bradshaw was "the one" for Mr. Big, furniture designer Aidan Shaw (played by John Corbett) thought she was the only one for him. "When women tell me they like *Sex and the City*, I always ask them one question: Big or Aidan?" says King. "And you can tell who the woman is by how she responds to that question. There are women who really like Mr. Big, because he's challenging, he's aspirational. He's the one you can't get. And then there are women who prefer Aidan. Aidan was loving and sexy and supportive, and he couldn't get enough of Carrie."

Unfortunately for Aidan, he wasn't "the one" for Carrie. But in all great failed love stories there will always be a connection to the feelings of the past. "Carrie Bradshaw probably felt her most desired when she was around him," says King, "and in the sequel, Carrie starts remembering who she was as a single person, and of course that opens the door to Aidan." So will the past stay in the past? "I put him in the Middle East," says King, "just for the trouble of it and for the thrill of seeing him again—the one she didn't choose."

Says Parker: "Words cannot describe the incredibly special and gifted person that is John Corbett. There's an ease to his work that may make people think that the role of Aidan comes to him really easily, but he works as hard as anybody."

and introducing

MAX RYAN AS RIKARD SPIRT

For Samantha, losing her hormones and her sex drive is an unthinkable nightmare that seems like it could come true—until she catches the eye of sexy Danish architect Rikard Spirt, played by British action star Max Ryan. According to Ryan, joining the cast of *Sex and the City* was a welcome change. "I've been playing the bad guy for quite a few years now, so I was like, This is great—I'm not killing anybody or being killed!" Rikard is just the cure for what's ailing Samantha, but an evening with him could end up more trouble than it's worth.

THE BUTLERS

For their all-expenses-paid seven-star trip to the Arab Emirates, no luxury is spared—including a personal butler for each of the ladies. The four young men assigned to them are everything you'd imagine a butler to be: courteous, helpful, and kind—and in the case of Samantha's butler, Abdul, possessing certain secret qualities. But it's Carrie's butler, Garau, who ends up helping the most. "The two have a special bond, and they have a conversation about what it is to be married and what life

with another person in the world is like," says British actor Raza Jaffrey, who also became a big fan of working with the ladies: "Even when they walked over sand dunes in high heels, they kept their sense of humor about them."

MILEY CYRUS AS HERSELF
"I thought, What's the biggest cream pie I can throw at Samantha?" remembers Michael Patrick King. "And then I thought, Miley Cyrus in the same dress. A fifty-two-year-old and a seventeen-year-old in the same dress says something." Fortunately, Miley was a *Sex and the City* and fashion fan and didn't need much convincing to come on board. When she was done filming, she didn't get to keep the dress,

but, according to Cyrus, "I did get to keep the necklace. It's like these giant spikes, and I wanted to wear it when I was performing, but my mom said, 'That would be dangerous. You can't wear that on stage!'"

PENÉLOPE CRUZ AS CARMEN
In the script, there is a moment where Mr. Big needs to be a little bad. Says King, "He has to be bad because he's the big bad wolf from the series. So I thought, What can I do to make one moment where you see the old flirtatious Mr. Big? I needed somebody who would make an impact." No one makes more of an impact than Oscar-winning Spanish superstar Penelope Cruz, who also happened to be a loyal *Sex and the City* fan.

RON WHITE AS MIRANDA'S BOSS

Even though his cameo is brief, fans and non-fans alike will undoubtedly appreciate Blue Collar Comedy Tour veteran comedian Ron White's acerbic style. Playing Miranda's no-nonsense new boss, he proves he's just the man to push Miranda's buttons. "I wanted someone who was original, male, and whom feminists would hate immediately," says Michael Patrick King.

TIM GUNN AS HIMSELF

Joining the cast for a red-carpet cameo was *Project Runway* mentor and fashion guru Tim Gunn. "I felt like a kid in a candy store," he says of the experience. "From my point of view, *Sex and the City* is really what created a fervor in America for all things fashion."

NOAH MILLS AS NICKY

Samantha is single and back on the market, and after a night with Anthony's hot brother, Nicky, played by Noah Mills, everyone at the hotel knows it.

ALICE EVE AS ERIN

Joining Charlotte's growing family is a new Irish nanny, Erin, played by actress Alice Eve. Erin has been brought in to help Charlotte with Lily and Rose, and Charlotte sees her as a lifesaver—patient, loving, well educated—until Samantha lays eyes on her. And just like that, "well educated" is overshadowed by "well endowed," leaving Charlotte to wonder just how much of a threat a double-D nanny is to her happy home.

LIZA MINNELLI AS HERSELF

"As I was writing the script, I typed 'Liza Minnelli,' thinking, Maybe . . . but could we get her?" explains King. Fortunately, Liza was game and ready to play along. "It was amazing that we got her and were able to pull it off," says producer John Melfi.

"At the end she said to me, 'When you're finished with me, give me the mike. I have a little surprise for you all,'" remembers King, "So I said, 'Ladies and gentlemen, that's a wrap on Liza Minnelli,' and everybody went crazy, and they pulled out her *Sex and the City* director's chair with LIZA MINNELLI on the back. And she sat down and said, 'Even though it's only been a week, I feel like we've been together a very long time. So here's a song my mother and father used to say represented show business.' And she sang 'Ev'ry Time We Say Goodbye.'

"There's was a hush over the crowd as she was singing it, and we had four swans swimming around in a moat around the dance floor. For a week, those swans never once attempted to get out of their moat. But as she was singing, we watched as one of the swans swam over, got out of the moat, climbed out, and walked over to her. And then another one got out. They walked over to her feet, and she just said, 'Oh, they like music.' She didn't even stop. This swan sat at her feet and watched her as she finished the song. We were all stunned. Later, Kristin Davis said to me, 'Of course they got out. It was her swan song.'"

the
fashion

The latest chapter presented some special new challenges as well as a unique opportunity. "I had a lot of fun with this movie, because it took us away on a magic vacation," says Patricia Field. "I could step up and use that as a jumping board to really make the clothing gorgeous and not worry about reality so much."

If Field was ready to step up, the world of fashion was more than ready to help. Weeks before the fittings took place, she and Molly Rogers were inundated by designers eager to see their work on the big screen. "There was so much clothing. We had a shoe room with just shoes and a room with shelves and shelves of bags. We had racks of clothing in a huge space like a gymnasium, really. We had two rooms just for jewelry—fine jewelry and costume jewelry. The whole world of fashion was in those rooms. It was like going into a department store."

the wardrobe room

"To have racks and racks of clothes from every important and emerging designer in the world . . . it was an alternate universe," adds Sarah Jessica Parker. "It couldn't have been further from where we started."

"The great fireworks display is Carrie's closet," says Michael Patrick King, "but there are a lot of real nuts and bolts to what Pat does, and in this movie she also had to go to a whole other hemisphere of clothing."

The "other hemisphere"—literally the Eastern Hemisphere—presented the new challenge of how to bring the "Sex" to the Middle East. Islamic culture values modesty above all else in matters of dress. And outside of the more permissive hotel environments, women are expected to carry themselves more demurely, covering their breasts, legs, stomach, and shoulders as a sign of respect. "Pat would say, 'I have to show the shoulders!'" says King, "so

she started to invent all of these shoulder capes and shawls."

For research, Pat and Molly traveled to Dubai. "We had never been there before," says Pat. "We saw what was going to be our backdrop, and I was able to weave it into my fantasy of four girls from New York going over there in high style."

"Every color or ethnic sparkle that she could put in the movie, she did," says King. The attention to detail is not lost on the show's sophisticated audience. Says Field, "Wherever I go in the world, people come up to me and they know me, and they tell me about all of their experiences with *Sex and the City*: It's kind of a

worldwide exclusive club of millions of females. It's an amazing experience. And that's the most thrilling thing to me about having worked on this project."

"People always ask me, How are you going to outdo yourself next?" says Field. "Because people are expecting and anticipating." She continues, "But really that is not my reality at all. If I had some kind of consciousness of other people's expectations, it would freeze me up and make me miserable and not allow me to be creative and have fun with it. I would be worrying about what everybody thinks, and that is not part of the process for me."

G5

SHOPPING @ BERGDORF

WADDING

CONNECTICUT

LOOK GROUPINGS
FOR SCENES WITH
ALL FOUR WOMEN

METM 5 AHMED

AMINE CASTING 7

HM ST 2 YOUSSEF

HM ST 4 REDA

Bell Captain 1

HMC 2 MOUNIR

WARDROBE ROOM IN MOROCCO

PATRICIA FIELD MODELS TOM BINNS LAMINATED MAGAZINE COLLAGE JEWELS

DRESSER JOSEPH LA CORTE HELPS SJP WITH A CLASP

CARRIE 01

PRODUCER JOHN MELFI HELPS OUT AND MODELS A BUTLER UNIFORM

51

what
carrie
wore

Since *Sex and the City* began, Carrie Bradshaw has been the most fashionably daring character. But it wasn't always so simple to come up with fresh and effortless looks in the early days. "We couldn't get anybody to loan us a sock for twenty-four hours back then," says Sarah Jessica Parker. "That's what was so incredible about Pat Field—she was so industrious and smart and creative. She would see the way New York really was at that time but use vintage as a big part of Carrie's wardrobe, which really established who Carrie was. Part of it was just a necessity, but it was also a design choice."

Carrie may be the picture of timeless fashion, but that wasn't always the case for Parker. "I personally made as many bad choices as anybody else in the '80s, but I don't really regret it because it was age appropriate, and I think it's good to spend time trying to fit in and then realizing how unimportant it is," recalls Parker. "You have to try to be like everybody else to understand how incredibly satisfying it is to not be like everybody else."

For this film, the challenges of not showing too much skin while the girls are in the Middle East presented some fun new opportunities. "We ended up wearing a lot of long dresses. There was a huge amount of beautiful dresses from the Halston archive that were long and simple, and they perfectly suited this very cinematic, very exotic, very colorful backdrop." Herewith, Parker takes us through every outfit she wears in the film.

MYKITA

SOLANGE AZAGURY-PARTRIDGE

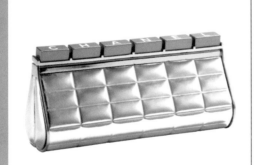

CHANEL

CHRISTIAN LOUBOUTIN

"There were two dresses in contention for the movie's opening shot. I'm so glad this dress came out the winner."

HALSTON

TAFFETA FABRIC

"I had the idea to get a bolt of taffeta and distress it— wanted it to look like it was at the bottom of Carrie's purse. Tied it myself."

"Interestingly, it's difficult to find the correct width of these bracelets from this period."

VINTAGE

VINTAGE

"I used a safety pin to attach it."

VINTAGE

"These shoes worked more than once."

BRIAN ATWOOD

"Hardest outfit to figure out, took about three fittings to get it right."

"Early 'Roger'"

dress: LAURA ASHLEY
corset: BETSEY JOHNSON
shirt: VINTAGE AMY BARR
bra: CHANTELLE

"From a thrift shop."

"I cut the neck myself."

CONVERSE

sweatshirt: VINTAGE
jeans: JORDACHE

"*Since this is a flashback, I thought I should put my mole back.*"

"*I think I cut it too much.*"

"There was another headpiece that we all responded to. We felt we needed a 'Carrie' touch. Our first choice was 'burned' by someone else. (In Pat Field vernacular, 'burn' is defined as someone else got their hands on it first.) Our good fortune, it turns out, as this was a far more unusual one."

TRIVIÁL

"Can fit a sum total of three pieces of Bazooka and three cough drops."

CHANEL

"Very special new designer."

CHARLOTTE OLYMPIA

"Exactly what we hoped the tuxedo as scripted would be."

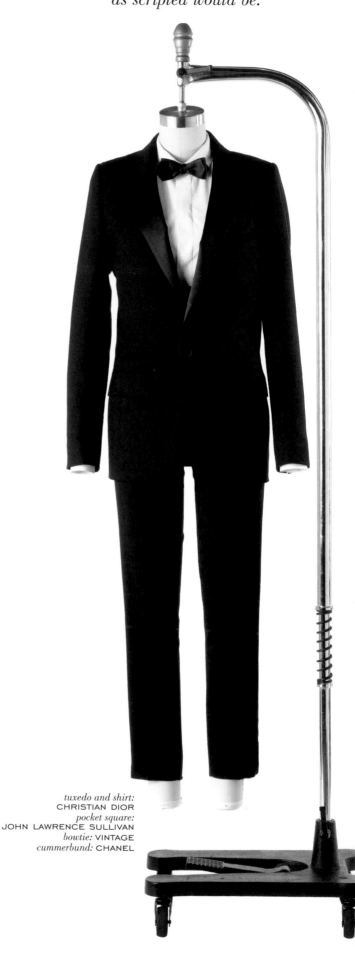

tuxedo and shirt:
CHRISTIAN DIOR
pocket square:
JOHN LAWRENCE SULLIVAN
bowtie: VINTAGE
cummerbund: CHANEL

MYKITA

VINTAGE

"Animal print? This a Carrie first."

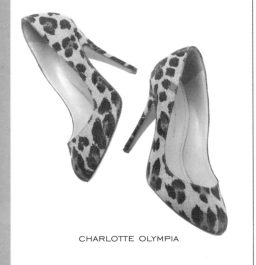

CHARLOTTE OLYMPIA

"This is a very old-school Carrie outfit, nothing really 'goes together.'"

"I loved this skirt, and we tried dozens of tops."

shirt: ZARA
skirt: VINTAGE
bra: COSABELLA

"Originally a vintage pair of cuffs from Seedhouse— I only wore one."

VINTAGE SEEDHOUSE

shirt: BALMAIN
skirt: AZZEDINE ALAÏA

MANOLO BLAHNIK

63

CHANEL

"Since I couldn't find a place to wear this hat in the movie, I at least got to hold it."

JEE VICE

JIMMY CHOO

CHRISTIAN LOUBOUTIN

"The 'Rebellious Spectator'— that's what I named these."

CHRISTIAN LOUBOUTIN

CHAHAN

"Vintage belt peeking out."

dress: HALSTON
belt: VINTAGE

"Pat just loved this dress."

SOLANGE AZAGURY-PARTRIDGE

"Pat brought this home from Turkey."

UNKNOWN

"We tried on about six pairs of shoes for this look."

CHRISTIAN DIOR

"The men's tie we threw on in the fitting."

dress: THE ROW
tie: LANVIN
bra: COSABELLA

KIMBERLY
MCDONALD

jumpsuit: BALMAIN
cape: MAISON MARTIN MARGIELA

BALMAIN BELT

CHARLES JOURDAN

GIUSEPPE ZANOTTI

"Pat and Molly found this in Paris."

CHAHAN

ADRIANA CASTRO

PIERRE HARDY

dress: JOANNA MASTROIANNI

CALVIN KLEIN

LOW LUV

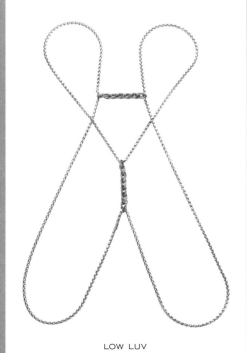

PERRIN

*"These are the same shoes
I wear with the first '80s outfit."*

BRIAN AIWOOD

shirt and skort: ALEXANDER WANG
bra: LA FÉE VERTE
sunglasses: CALVIN KLEIN

"My gift for cast and crew, turned inside out."

"SEX AND THE CITY 2"
SOUVENIR SWEATBAND

"This is a 'Highline Bag.' Love it!"

SHELLY STEFFEE

BRIAN ATWOOD

"My own jeans. I wore them to set that day. Pat saw them, tossed previously set costume, ran and got a shirt from her store, and ten minutes later we were shooting."

shirt: VINTAGE
jeans: CLOSED

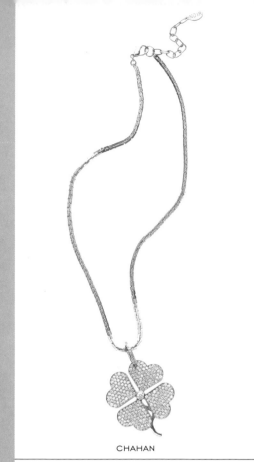

CHAHAN

BEA VALDES

CHRISTIAN LOUBOUTIN

"It made me very nervous to be back in this dress TEN YEARS later! We did it for the audience, and a nod to the past. It was hard to get my hands on it."

JOHN GALLIANO FOR DIOR

*"We always
wanted to do
this scene
in heels—
took some
convincing
for MPK
to agree."*

*"These shoes
were so pretty,
we really wanted
to find a spot
for them.
And we try to
get as many
shoes as possible
on-screen!"*

SALVATORE FERRAGAMO

jumpsuit: ALEXANDER WANG
belt: VINTAGE

*"Mandy wrapped my bun…
I asked Pat, Molly,
and Jessica to get lots
of scarves at the souk."*

romper: VINTAGE
slip: CALVIN KLEIN

RENÉ CAOVILLA

77

*"Well, what can you say?
When else will I
ever wear this in my life?"*

YOHJI YAMAMOTO

SOLANGE AZAGURY-PARTRIDGE

YSL

GIUSEPPE ZANOTTI

NORMA KAMALI

VINTAGE

CALVIN KLEIN

LOW LUV

ADRIANA CASTRO

*"We worked with Manolo
to create these beloved shoes.
I called them 'The Cage.'"*

MANOLO BLAHNIK

*"I spent days in this outfit and I loved it.
Even on day 70."*

HALSTON

*"Look for this bracelet again.
Too good to use only once."*

MARK WALSH / LESLIE CHIN
FOR RODARTE

VBH

*"Another Manolo designed
just for SATC 2. Very lucky."*

MANOLO BLAHNIK

*"I wish this outfit had more screen time.
It's quintessential Carrie and I adored it."*

RODRIGO
OTAZU

jumpsuit: LEONARD
vest: MICHAEL & HUSHI

"Could we find a way to work these sunglasses?"

CHANEL

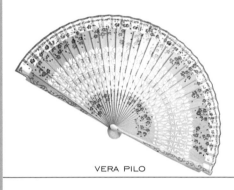

ANDREA LIEBERMAN

VERA PILO

VINTAGE

"Another special Manolo designed just for SATC 2."

MANOLO BLAHNIK

"If I had to pick a favorite…"

"A way to cover shoulders."

J'ADORE DIOR 8

blouse and skirt: ZAC POSEN
shirt: CHRISTIAN DIOR

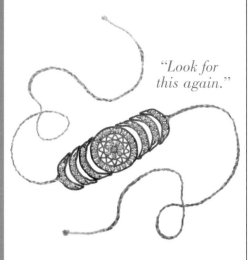

"Look for this again."

VINTAGE

CALVIN KLEIN

ANDREA LIEBERMAN

SOLANGE AZAGURY-PARTRIDGE

"Opal. My son's birthstone."

"Another Manolo designed expressly for SATC 2."

MANOLO BLAHNIK

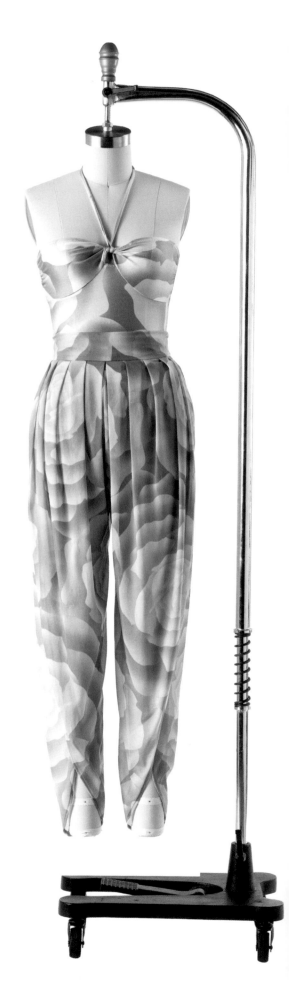

GIDEON OBERSON

*"These shoes
couldn't be seen—
so I did the
next best thing."*

ANTIK BATIK

"Look for this bracelet again."

LOW LUV

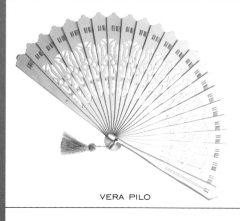

VERA PILO

"Hard to stand and walk on sand in these shoes—I didn't care."

CIUSEPPF ZANOTTI

"The designer wrote to me. That's how we met, and ultimately her jewelry ended up in the movie."

SHOUROUK

"I named this jacket 'Rum Raisin.' We loved it, and you'll see it quite a bit in the movie."

jacket: MAISON MARTIN MARGIELA
slip and pants: JOHN GALLIANO
handkerchief: YSL

PHILIP TREACY

"I believe Molly brought these to me when I was on the camel. She always has a surprise from what she calls her 'Snack Pack.'"

VINTAGE

LOW LUV

HERMÈS

"I climbed a sand dune in these over and over and over..."

YSL

blouse: ZARA
bustier: DIOR
pants: RALPH LAUREN

90

RODRIGO OTAZU

"We loved this dress. Its place in the movie kept changing 'til we settled on the most perfect scene for it."

"Purse tossed in at the last minute to hold BlackBerry."

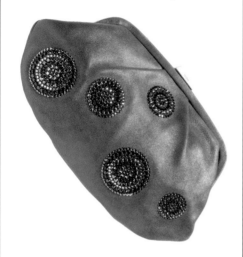

RODO

"These were copied from a pair I found in Turkey."

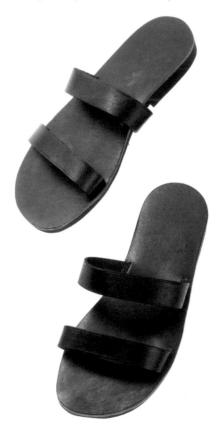

BARBARA SHAUM

HALSTON

"Here it is again."

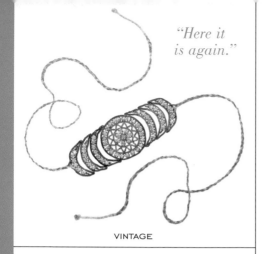

VINTAGE

KIMBERLY MCDONALD

RAVEN KAUFFMAN

"Danced in these shoes for days and days. Beat them up!"

CHRISTIAN LOUBOUTIN

"These are Closed jeans, but Phillipe & David Blond did the bleaching, distressing, and bejeweling."

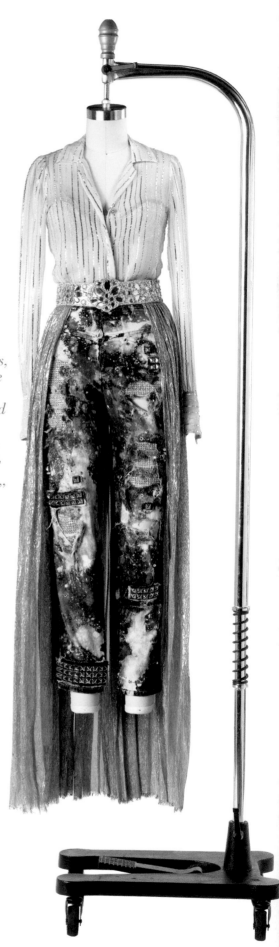

blouse: STELLA MCCARTNEY
jeans: CLOSED
skirt: CHANEL

MARK WALSH/LESLIE
CHIN FOR RODARTE

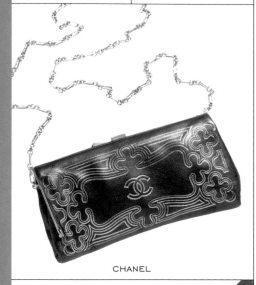

EYE CANDY

CHANEL

"The finishing touch."

ZAC POSEN

"Perhaps one of the most amazing pairs of shoes I have ever worn."

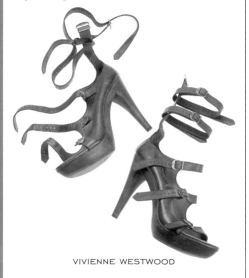

VIVIENNE WESTWOOD

"Second favorite outfit."

UNKNOWN

"Rum Rais Again. It just kept being right."

dress: PUCCI
jacket: MAISON MARTIN MARGIELA

COCOTAY

TRIVIÁL

"It's a ridiculous hat for the desert, but that never stopped us. I couldn't wear it, so it was set dressed near me."

BEA VALDES

MANOLO BLAHNIK

dress: HALSTON
tank: STELLA MCCARTNEY
belt: REEM ACRA

VINTAGE

"So many beautiful fans to choose from."

VERA PILO

ALEXANDER WANG

BRIAN ATWOOD

SOLANGE AZAGURY-PARTRIDGE

"Rum Raisin!"

"We stuffed two pocket squares in for extra color."

dress: HALSTON
jacket: MAISON MARTIN MARGIELA
pocket squares: YSL

ALBERTUS SWANEPOEL

HERMÈS

MANOLO BLAHNIK

RALPH LAUREN

102

"A spectacular dress."

STEPHEN DWECK

dress: LANVIN

104

CHANEL

VINTAGE SEEDHOUSE

"Pat and I went into our archives and pulled all of our Manolos from the period in which we shot the series. We had these made based on a pair that belonged to Pat."

MANOLO BLAHNIK

top and pants: HALSTON

"My own black top from the first or second season of the series."

jacket: VINTAGE CHRISTIAN DIOR
jeans: CLOSED

"The first pair of shoes I tried on in the fittings. They were too small— didn't care. Mark Agnes stretched them as much as was possible. They still hurt— didn't care."

VINTAGE CHARLES JOURDAN

left earring:
KIMBERLY McDONALD

*"Two pairs, both just beautiful.
I thought, Well, I'll just wear
one of each. It's a solution."*

right earring: SOLANGE
AZAGURY-PARTRIDGE

JUDITH LIEBER

CHAHAN

CHARLOTTE OLYMPIA

DOLCE & GABBANA

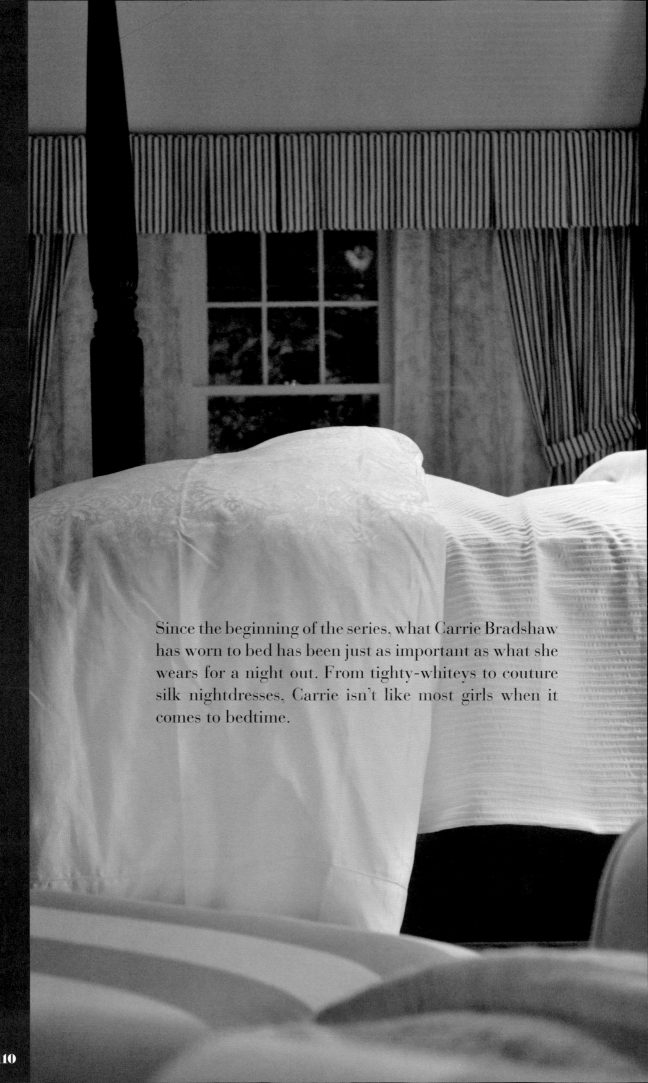

Since the beginning of the series, what Carrie Bradshaw has worn to bed has been just as important as what she wears for a night out. From tighty-whiteys to couture silk nightdresses, Carrie isn't like most girls when it comes to bedtime.

VINTAGE CALVIN KLEIN   CURVE

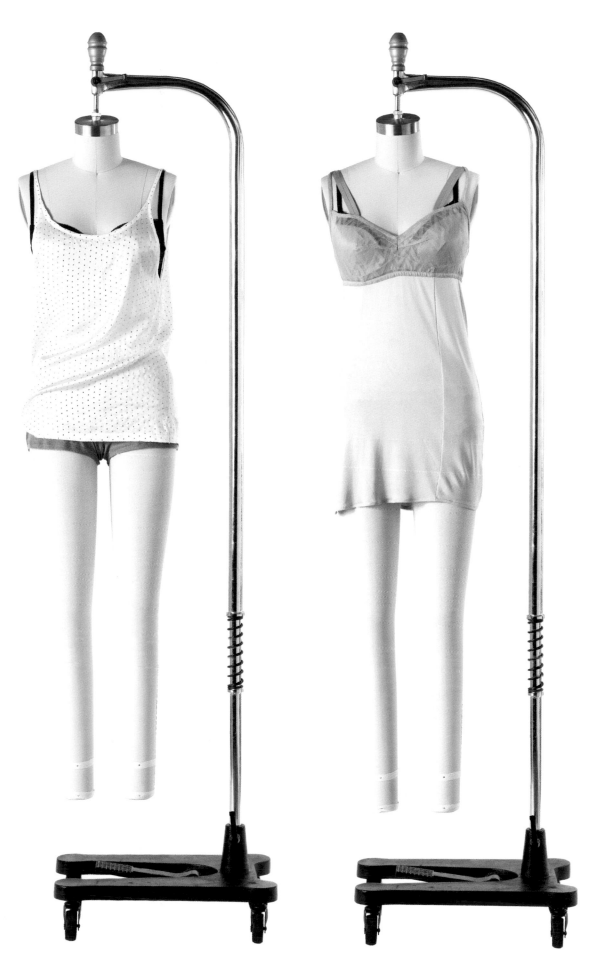

top: BALMAIN
bra: CALVIN KLEIN
shorts: HANRO

slip: THE LAKE & STARS
bra: HUIT

113

LOW LUV

GIANVITO
ROSSI

CARINE GILSON

ODETTE BARSA

dressing gown: YIGAL AZOURËL
bra: ERES
underwear: ERES

nightgown: VINTAGE
bra: MARLIES DEKKERS
underwear: ON GOSSAMER

115

killed outfits

By the time Patricia Field and Sarah Jessica Parker had decided on the forty-two looks that Carrie wears in this film, Parker had tried on and rejected hundreds of outfits. "There are a lot of reasons why things don't look good on me," says Parker. "In a way, it's one of the most fun parts, because it's very amusing to see something really awful on yourself." Herewith, a special look at Parker trying on the looks that didn't make the cut.

THESE VINTAGE BLUE SHOES WERE A KEEPER

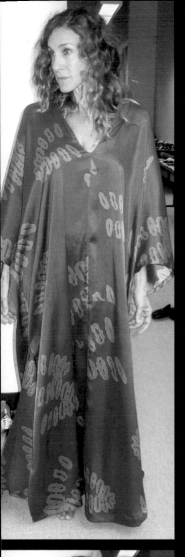

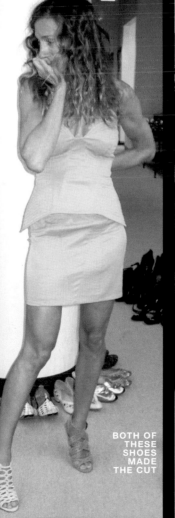

BOTH OF
THESE
SHOES
MADE
THE CUT

what samantha wore

"Samantha's like light or sound," says Patricia Field. "She just gets bigger and more crazy and out-rageous—crazy in a good way, of course." In keeping with her personality, Samantha has always been styled the most boldly of the four. "The costumes are so colorful and over the top," says Kim Cattrall. "But this time, there are fewer huge, chunky earrings and rings for Samantha. The chunky jewelry was replaced by focusing on Samantha's finger- and toenails. Each costume change was accompanied by another original creation by the brilliant nail designer Naomi Yasuda, whose clients include Alicia Keys." One piece of statement jewelry *did* make it into the movie, however. "One day I was walking down Madison Avenue past a jewelry store, and I saw this ring," say Field. "It was like a headlight, a big diamond. It stopped me in my tracks." It was no wonder. The price tag? $4.9 million. The jeweler agreed to lend the ring to Field, and it arrived with its own full-time security guard. Thankfully the ring made it back without incident.

dress: NAEEM KHAN
shoes: PATRICIA FIELD
bag: VALENTINO
clutch: JIMMY CHOO
bracelet: MIMI SO
ring: NOIR

119

dress: ITEM *shoes:* PATRICIA FIELD
bag: VBH *sunglasses:* PAUL SMITH

vest: LEVI'S *shirt:* NATASHA
pants: MICHI *shoes:* FANTASY
bag: PATRICIA FIELD

dress: ROBERTO CAVALLI
bracelet: FARAONE MENNELLA

dress: RICK OWENS
shoes: SERGIO ROSSI
thong: MARLIES DEKKERS
ring: TOM BINNS

dress: MATTHEW WILLIAMSON
belt: DAVID SAMUEL MENKES
necklace: NOIR   *bracelet:* TIFFANY

dress: MARC BAUER
earrings: RODRIGO OTAZU
bracelet: DANNIJO

121

dress: GRAEME BLACK
earrings and bracelet: NOIR

bathing suit and wrap: BALIZZA
shoes. RENÉ CAOVILLA
sunglasses: ROBERTO CAVALLI

dress: JEAN PAUL GAULTIER
wrap: BALIZZA   *hat:* HORST
bag: RALPH LAUREN

jumpsuit: MAISON MARTIN MARGIELA
wrap: BALIZZA
necklace: SIMON ALCANTARA

dress: MARC BAUER *belt:* CACHÉ
shoes: VIKTOR & ROLF
scarf: ROBERTO CAVALLI
earrings: VINTAGE

jumpsuit: DIANE VON FURSTENBERG
wrap: BALIZZA
belt: STREET AHEAD

123

dress: THE BLONDS
belt: VINTAGE
earrings: NICOLE ROMANO
ring: LE VIVE

robe: LIZ CLAIBORNE
turban: CANYON ROSE

jacket: LANVIN *shirt:* REEM ACRA
shorts: ROBERTO CAVALLI
bracelet: KARA ROSS *ring:* ALEXIS BITTAR

dress: MATTHEW AMES
cape: THIERRY MUGLER
belt: MELAMED
earrings and ring: DIOR

125

what charlotte wore

"I love Charlotte's taste because it's a little more conservative," says Kristin Davis. "I wear a Dior suit at the beginning of the movie—perfectly Charlotte and perfectly wonderful." Charlotte may have evolved from preppy Connecticut girl to tasteful Upper East Side mom, but Kristin's own journey took a slight detour during her formative years. Says Davis, "I was a Southern preppy, but I went to school at Rutgers, in New Jersey. When I first arrived, my friends were like, 'You can't dress like that,'" she remembers. "So they took me to a Salvation Army, where I got a vintage men's jacket. I wore it like Madonna did, but I was a little more low key than that."

But there's nothing low key about the latest movie. "When you go on a trip to a foreign country, you often change how you look, and you adjust to the environment you're in, and you might actually have a little fun with it." That was certainly the case for the trip the girls take in this film. "It's a brighter movie this time because of the trip," says Kristin. "The clothes are brighter, the scenery is brighter. Everything is like it's in Technicolor."

louse: L'WREN SCOTT
irt: VALENTINO
pron: ANTHROPOLOGIE
hoes: CHRISTIAN LOUBOUTIN

suit: DIOR
shoes: CHRISTIAN LOUBOUTIN
bag: DIOR watch: KAYRITA
earrings: VAN CLEEF & ARPELS

blouse: STRENESSE
sweater and skirt: LILY PULITZER
shoes: TRETORN
bag: VINTAGE

dress: OSCAR DE LA RENTA
ring: POMELLATO

dress: ROBERT DANES

dress: OSCAR DE LA RENTA
bag: SALVATORE FERRAGAMO
earrings: HARMON MILANO
bracelet: SYDNEY EVAN ring: MIMI SO

dress: THIERRY MUGLER
bag: CARLOS FALCHI
bracelets: CARTIER

suit: GIANFRANCO FERRÉ
scarf: CHANEL earrings: CARTIER

dress: JOANNA MASTROIANNI scarves: REEM ACRA
belt: GIANFRANCO FERRÉ shoes: PIERRE HARDY

dress: LANVIN
headband: CHANEL

dress: VINTAGE *belt:* CHANEL *scarf:* JULIEN DAVID
shoes: MIU MIU *hat:* PATRICIA UNDERWOOD
bracelets: CARTIER *luggage:* LOUIS VUITTON

top: ALEXANDER WANG *caftan:* PATRICIA FIELD
pants: ZAC POSEN *belt:* BILL BLASS
hat: VIVIENNE WESTWOOD

bathing suit: ROSA CHÁ *wrap:* MARC BAUER
hat: PATRICIA UNDERWOOD
necklace: JENNIFER FISHER

dress: ALEXANDER MCQUEEN
wrap: VINTAGE *bracelet:* VINTAGE
earrings: FARAONE MENNELLA

dress: VINTAGE *necklace:* CHANEL
bracelet: RODRIGO OTAZU
shoes: CHRISTIAN LOUBOUTIN

dress: YSL
earrings: BLU BY BETTY LOU MOSCOT
bracelet: JACK VARTANIAN

blouse: ROBERTO CAVALLI

dress: THOMAS MAIER sweater: YIGAL AZROUËL
shoes: CASADEI

jumpsuit: VINTAGE scarf: REEM ACRA
bracelet: TIFFANY

dress: MICHAEL KORS
sweater: J. CREW
luggage: LOUIS VUITTON

skirt: MICHAEL KORS
shoes: YSL *necklace:* JENNIFER FISHER

dress: OSCAR DE LA RENTA
shoes: BRIAN ATWOOD
necklace: JENNIFER FISHER

what miranda wore

"At the beginning of the TV show, Miranda really had no interest in fashion," says Patricia Field. But as Miranda became more successful and relaxed, her cynical, type-A personality softened—and so did her look, evolving into something more comfortable and sexy. Now, "Miranda has the money for the haircut and the clothes and the shoes and the bag," says Cynthia Nixon, "and I think you can see it on her." When Miranda takes her refined tastes to the Middle East, she adopts the new role of fashion police—patrolling Samantha's natural instinct to show off her skin in the conservative Muslim world. "[In this film], we still have our fashion-forward sensibility, but it has to be realistic," says Cynthia. "We weren't dressed provocatively in the Middle East. Miranda, in particular, had done a lot of research and was very up to speed on the social mores."

dress: BOTTEGA VENETA
shoes: CHRISTIAN LOUBOUTIN
bracelet: ALEXIS BITTAR

suit: VINTAGE
blouse: NORDSTROM
shoes: REEBOK

dress: JULIEN MACDONALD
shoes: DIOR *bag:* CHANEL

dress: ZERO + MARIA CORNEJO
belt: REID & REID

romper: BCBG
necklace: VINTAGE

dress: MATTHEW AMES *jacket:* RACHEL ROY
earrings: JACK VARTANIAN

jumpsuit: VINTAGE *shoes:* RALPH LAUREN
sunglasses: JEE VICE
earrings: SAMANTHA WILLS

dress: ROBERTO CAVALLI
belt: VINTAGE
shoes: RENÉ CAOVILLA
bag: JIL SANDER

UNKNOWN

bathing suit: ERES wrap: ROBERTO CAVALLI
head scarf: JOHN DAVID earrings: ALEXIS BITTAR

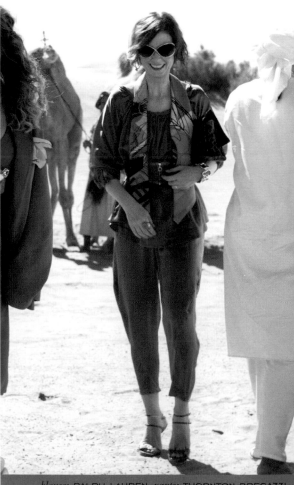

blouse: RALPH LAUREN pants: THORNTON BREGAZZI
scarf: CHANEL belt: MISSONI shoes: JIMMY CHOO
bag: LOUIS VUITTON sunglasses: TOM FORD

dress: HERMÈS *jacket:* ELIZABETH AND JAMES
shoes: RALPH LAUREN *bag:* CALVIN KLEIN
bracelet: ROBERTO CAVALLI
earrings: PEPITO

dress: HERMÈS *pants:* MISSONI
belt: ROBERTO CAVALLI
shoes: SALVATORE FERRAGAMO *hat:* HERMÈS

dress: MARA HOFFMAN
bracelet: ROBERTO CAVALLI

dress: HALSTON
belt: VINTAGE
shoes: RALPH LAUREN

jacket: BILL BLASS
blouse: YSL *pants:* PUCCI
sunglasses: JEE VICE

jacket: DOMA *blouse:* ARMANI
jeans: LEVI'S

drss: JOANNA MASTROIANNI
bracelet: NOIR
earrings: GASIA

dress: ROLAND MOURET

dress: DONNA KARAN
earrings: MASHA ARCHER

sets
and the
cities

shooting in new york

Before the ladies take their first-class trip abroad, they reunite in the city where they first met as twentysomething girls. On the second day of shooting, the crew recreated 1980s New York at the intersection of Fifth Avenue and 58th Street by giving it a head-to-toe makeover. "We had to work with the city and close down part of Fifth Avenue to pull it off," says producer John Melfi. "And to really sell it, we brought in dozens of period cars and hundreds of extras in 80s costumes."

Add to that a hundred-person crew, an army of trucks carrying tons of equipment, swarms of paparazzi, and hundreds of onlookers, and you get the challenge of filming on the streets of Manhattan. Even a less ambitious scene can require months of preparation. Explains Melfi, "Carrie and Big's apartment is supposed to be located in a pretty tony building of

the Upper East Side. It took months to secure just that one location. We had meetings with the city, every resident in the building had to give their approval, the street had to be closed, and buses had to be rerouted."

But one location remains unchanged after all these years: Carrie's old apartment. Her Upper East Side brownstone isn't really located on the Upper East Side, but in fact far downtown in Greenwich Village. And it was there, shooting the second film, that the crew witnessed a first—the *Sex and the City* tour group stumbling upon the movie set. "They just kind of swarmed over us," remembers Melfi. "It was surreal to be shooting while people were getting off the *Sex and the City* bus. It was overwhelming to be part of this cultural moment."

Other locations were a little more manageable to recreate, such as the iconic SoHo coffee shop set from the series. The original set seen in so many episodes was actually built on a soundstage at Silvercup Studios in Queens. But for the films, the coffee shop was recreated if not for real, then in the real world—in an empty furniture store in SoHo.

MIRANDA'S
OFFICE

SAMANTHA'S OFFICE
IN TIMES SQUARE

The crew would go on to film in a dozen other iconic
locations, such as Bergdorf Goodman department store and
the legendary Ziegfeld Theatre. But perhaps the most surpris-
ing makeover came when it was time to choose a location for
Samantha's office.

"I wanted it to be electric and busy—like her energy," says
Michael Patrick King, "It had to show that she was connected
and in the center of it all." The right location turned out to be
the newly restored Renaissance Hotel overlooking the heart of
Times Square. Her office is actually the hotel's main restaurant.
Production designer Jeremy Conway simply took out the tables
and chairs and added walls.

OUTSIDE THE PLAZA HOTEL

THE MODEL

BUILDING THE SET

THE WEDDING CHINA

BEFORE SHOOTING

LIVE SWANS

the wedding set

The design team topped even themselves to create the big white wedding that opens the movie. Says Michael Patrick King, "The wedding is stylish in a way that you don't see anymore. It has a very old Hollywood feel to it. The scenery is extravagant: it's a huge exterior built indoors. And even the wedding motif is in black and white, so there are times when it actually looks like something out of *Top Hat* or a Preston Sturges movie. It's in color, but we deliberately stressed the black and white."

Over two months on a soundstage in Brooklyn, production designer Jeremy Conway and a crew of hundreds of carpenters, painters, and craftspeople re-created the rustic colonial courtyard of a quaint country inn—and then transformed that quaint inn into one outrageous, snow-white, crystal-covered party. "Sparkle was a very important part of this set," says set decorator Lydia Marks. "We managed to add sparkle into the flower arrangements, into the trees, into the handrails on the footbridges—pretty much anywhere we could put crystals."

"You haven't seen a set like that since MGM in 1935," says Mario Cantone, who plays Charlotte's wedding-planner friend, Anthony Marantino. "I mean, it's literally like a Busby Berkeley musical."

THE WEDDING CAKE

The Inn at Drake Point

carrie & big's apartment

Carrie and Big have finally settled down and moved into a very chic Fifth Avenue apartment not far from 245 East 73rd Street, the home of Carrie's former single self. Carrie's old apartment is back for a cameo—meticulously reconstructed by Jeremy Conway and his team—but Conway's biggest challenge was designing the set that would become Carrie and Big's home together. "I think we spent more time on this space than on anything else in the film," he says.

THROW PILLOWS:
CALYPSO HOME,
THE RUG COMPANY,
AND HOME & ABROAD

PAINTING:
SATC 2 ART DEPARTMENT

SOFA: MONTAUK SOFA

RUG:
THE RUG COMPANY

CHANDELIER:
LINDSEY ADELMAN
STUDIO

WALLPAPER:
HOLLAND & SHERRY

VASE: PROPERTY

DOME: CENTER44 ANTIQUES

TILE: HEATH CERAMIC

PENDANT LIGHT:
JOHN SALIBELLO
ANTIQUES

TABLE AND CHAIRS:
BAXTER AND LIEBCHEN

CABINETS:
HELLMAN-CHANG

RUG:
THE RUG COMPANY

CHANDELIER: PROPERTY

TABLE:
ALAN MOSS

CHINA:
BERNARDAUD

OTTOMAN:
ANNE KYYRÖ QUINN

"My thought, as the writer, was that Carrie decorated this place with a decorator who had a very keen eye as to what would make Big comfortable," says Michael Patrick King. "It's not Carrie Bradshaw—her redecorated apartment at the end of the last movie was all color and feminine, like a little girl's bedroom. And it's not Big's bachelor-life apartment, either, which was sort of modern and sharklike. The fun for me and for the design team was to figure out how Carrie would interpret her and Big as a couple."

CANE CHAIRS:
DUANE ANTIQUES

153

HEADBOARD:
JEREMY CONWAY,
SATC 2 ART DEPARTMENT

WALLPAPER:
LEE JOFA

LINENS:
ANICHINI

FLORAL DESIGN:
TESS CASEY,
AISLING FLOWERS

NIGHTSTANDS:
HELLMAN-CHANG

ARTWORK: ALICIA
BOCK, ISACK
KOUSNSKY STUDIO

CHAIR:
PROPERTY

TABLE: ABC CARPET & HOME

"To me, a lot of the furniture is very linear and very 'Big,'" says Lydia Marks. "With the rugs, I tried to bring in Carrie, so that the apartment would have this linear quality, with a little bit of Carrie everywhere underneath. The colors and the patterns bring some femininity into what would otherwise be a more masculine space."

Says King. "That's the detailing genius of Jeremy and Lydia. I only have to put it out there, and then I come to the set and see that it's better than I even expected. You asked for a couch and a desk, but you didn't ask for feathered coasters—that's a surprise. It's like a stocking stuffer on Christmas morning."

And even though the apartment is for the two of them, one space remains signature Carrie: the closet. "One side of the closet is Carrie, and the other side is Big," says Conway. "What I love about that, of course, is that there's not enough room for Carrie, so she has to come over to Big's side a little bit."

"The palette in this closet is very different from the palette in Carrie's old closet," adds Marks. It's really about Carrie's grown-up clothes. There are no tutus here."

CARRIE WAS
MARRIED IN
THESE BLUE
MANOLOS

WALL HANGING:
THE RUG COMPANY

CONSOLE:
DUANE ANTIQUES

THIS MIRROR IS FROM
THE ORIGINAL SERIES

STUFF: FLEA MARKETS AND VINTAGE SHOPS

SETTEES:
MARTIN ALBERT
INTERIORS

CHAIR:
KNOLL

BENCH:
ALAN MOSS

COFFEE TABLE:
ABC CARPET & HOME

carrie's old apartment

Even though Carrie and Big have settled down and finally share a home of their own, the reality of the tough New York City real estate market means that Carrie hasn't sold the apartment that was her home for years. Not much has changed since the big makeover in the last movie, except that Carrie doesn't come around much anymore—just to write (or to visit her clothes). Her old closet is full of signature Carrie outfits—ones that she hasn't brought into her new, grown up closet, like the Dior newsprint dress she first wore in Season 3 of the TV series, which makes a special cameo appearance in the movie sequel. "We had to dig deep into Sarah Jessica's personal archives to retrieve signature pieces from Carrie's old apartment," says associate producer Melinda Relyea.

CARRIE WORE THIS DRESS IN PARIS IN SEASON SIX OF THE SERIES

RUG:
THE RUG COMPANY

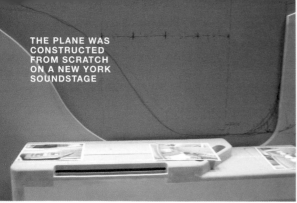

the airplane

When it came time to leave New York behind, the next task was reconstructing the luxury first-class cabin of the plane the ladies take to the Middle East. "We named the airline Afdal Air. *Afdal* is Arabic for 'smooth,'" explains Michael Patrick King. "So it's Smooth Air." Modeled on an Air Emirates Airbus A380, every detail of the plane cabin was replicated exactly—right down to the individual premiere suites. Also duplicated exactly was the plane's onboard first-class lounge bar, where the ladies help themselves to—what else?—Cosmos. Not re-created was the decadent onboard spa shower featured on many Emirates planes.

Welcome aboard

AK202
New York - Abu Dhabi/UAE

2E

Start
Go straight to
Movies & TV

THE FIRST-CLASS CABIN
FEATURED A WIDESCREEN
TELEVISION, PERSONAL
SNACK BASKET, AND
LIGHTED VANITY WITH
BVLGARI SPA PRODUCTS

shooting in morocco

When the crew finally landed in Morocco, a new set of design challenges presented itself: "We had to take Morocco and make it the Middle East," says Michael Patrick King. "Morocco is not the Middle East—it's an Islamic country, and it's exotic, but the Middle East is just different. So Jeremy Conway had to transform it, and it was a big task."

"Everything had to be shipped in—the Maybach cars, the wardrobe, the equipment," says John Melfi. "But Morocco has a seventy-five-year history of filmmaking. They really have a great crew base there." That crew immediately set to work on two key locations: the souk marketplace and the Taj Al-Sahara, "The Crown of the Desert," the fictional hotel that plays host to the ladies.

While the prepping crew was readying those locations, the shooting crew and the actors flew to Merzouga, a small town in the western Sahara Desert less than twenty miles from the Algerian border. "These days, people assume everything is green-screened and not real," says King. "But we were really there. We filmed on the same dunes where they filmed *Lawrence of Arabia*. It was a great, extravagant feat, and it added an enormous amount of energy to the production."

After a week in the Sahara, the cast and crew returned to Marrakech and began filming in the hotel and the old city for the next five weeks. "I think it's the best time we ever had as a group," says Sarah Jessica Parker. "I don't think we ever felt closer or more dependent upon each other in a really nice way."

"We were all in Morocco for Thanksgiving, and it felt very much like a family," says King. "We've been working together for twelve years, and as with a big family, when it's funny, it's really funny, and when it's stressful, it's really stressful. The idea of going to North Africa and putting four strangers on camels—the amount of time you'd need to earn that trust, you couldn't do it. But we can because we have that family feeling among us."

163

THE HOTEL GROUNDS WERE COMPLETELY
DESIGNED BY THE SATC 2 CREW,
SAVE FOR THE POOLSIDE CLUB, FILMED
AT NIKKI BEACH, MARRAKECH.

the hotel

Filming the exterior of the Mandarin Oriental Jnan Rahma Hotel, the actual hotel that stands in for the Taj Al-Sahara, presented yet another challenge: The Moroccan landscape is completely different from Abu Dhabi's. The hotel is located in the Palmeraie area of Marrakech, in an expanse of barren desert scrub with the Atlas Mountains rising in the distance. Abu Dhabi, meanwhile, is a coastal metropolis with a new and cosmopolitan skyline. Therefore, the coast and the city itself had to be digitally created and placed into the background in post-production.

Production chose the hotel because it had just been built and was not yet open to the public. The lack of guests ensured the crew unlimited access without disruption, but the lack of electricity and plumbing made shooting there a difficult challenge. With a little movie magic, though, the hotel became an extravagant Arabian jewel box.

BEDS: AND SO TO BED;
LINENS: ZARA HOME AND THE
WHITE COMPANY, LONDON

DINING TABLE TOP: INLAID MARBLE,
SOURCED LOCALLY IN MOROCCO;
ALL FURNITURE: FARLEY, UK;
SCREEN: SATC 2 ART DEPARTMENT

BATHROOM AND
HAMMERED BRASS
TUB: SATC 2 ART
DEPARTMENT;
TOWELS:
DES CHAMPS

THE ART DEPARTMENT
CALLED THIS
CHANDELIER "THE
JEWEL OF THE CROWN"

INTERIOR WALLS: FINISHED
IN CUSTOM-MIXED AND
DEEP-HUED VENETIAN
PLASTER JEWEL TONES

the karaoke club

For the hotel nightclub, Michael Patrick King was inspired by an elevated, circular dance floor he'd seen in a nightclub on his research trip to Dubai. "Anywhere in the world, it seems, there's a karaoke bar," he says. "I thought, What would a karaoke club be like in Abu Dhabi? Okay, we need go-go girls, but they should be belly dancers! So to me, it became this big production number. But the important thing was that the four girls were onstage singing 'I Am Woman' from a campy point of view—though in reality, that song is still relevant to different women in different parts of the world."

SHOOTING IN THE
MARRAKECH MEDINA,
FILLED WITH EXTRAS
AND CREW

the souk

Marrakech's Medina, or "old city," is a very tight, narrow series of alleyways, shops, streets, and workshops that dates back thousands of years. Throngs of people—residents and tourists alike—stream through by the thousands all day on foot, by donkey, and on mopeds. The Moroccan Medina is known worldwide as a place in which you can find almost anything and everything, and the locations department did their best to capture that atmosphere. Many of the locations picked were in some of the Medina's busiest streets, and therefore incredibly challenging to shoot in.

THIS ROOM WAS KNOWN AS "THE FORBIDDEN EXPERIENCE"

transportation

When the script called for four identical white luxury cars to chauffeur the ladies around on their desert vacation, John Melfi wondered, "How do I get four amazing, luxurious cars in the middle of the desert in another country?" The Maybach 62s turned out to be just the item—and fortunately four of them were available to lend to the production. With a price tag of over $500,000 each, getting them to the desert was a long, risky undertaking—the cars were air freighted from Los Angeles to Frankfurt, Germany, and then driven by road to Marrakech.

THIS FAKE CAMEL WAS ON STANDBY IN CASE THE REAL CAMELS DIDN'T COOPERATE WITH THE ACTORS—FORTUNATELY THEY DID

The cars weren't the only luxury item in the desert. Explains Melfi, "When Michael Patrick King returned from his research trip to Dubai, he said, 'Do you know there are good camels and there are not-so-good camels? We want the really good camels. We want the *Sex and the City* camels.' So we found these extraordinarily white camels that were perfect." The camels, however, were less than thrilled to make their silver-screen debut. "Camels are really sort of grumpy animals," says camel wrangler Cédric Proust. "They would never bite anyone or do anything wrong—they're just grumpy."

Sometimes you just have to get away with the girls.

credits

SPECIAL THANKS

Sarah Jessica Parker
Michael Patrick King
Melinda Relyea
Eric Cyphers

THANKS

Akhmiss Abdelmalek, Bouhasni Abdesselam, Craig Blankenhorn, Mario Cantone, Kim Cattrall, Joe Collins, Jeremy Conway, John Corbett, Miley Cyrus, Kristin Davis, Courtney D'Alesio, Cindy De La Hoz, David Eigenberg, Alice Eve, Ekta Farrar, Patricia Field, Willie Garson, Tim Gunn, Evan Handler, Craig Herman, Yoko Inoue, Raza Jaffrey, Coco Joly, Joseph La Corte, Tom Lappin, Thomas Liggett, Lydia Marks, Charlie Marroquin, John Melfi, Noah Mills, Liza Minnelli, David Mortimer, Lauren Nathan, Christopher Navratil, Marissa Neiman, Cynthia Nixon, Chris Noth, Emily Oberman, Elaine Piechowski, Jennifer Pinto, Max Ryan, Molly Rogers, Holly Rothman, Dave Rupert, Danny Santiago, Nathan Sayers, Ira Schreck, Victoria Selover, Bonnie Siegler, Lindsey Stanberry, Melanie Swartz, Emma Tait, Shoshana Thaler, Mark Walsh, Sydney Wasserman, Stephanie Wheeler, Ron White, and Jessica Zadnik

PHOTOGRAPHY CREDITS

All photographs by Craig Blankenhorn/ ™ & © New Line Productions, Inc., 2010 except for the following: Pages 20-21: Michael Patrick King; page 25, bottom right: Marissa Neiman; page 47: Nathan Sayers; page 49: Melinda Relyea; pages 50-51: Melinda Relyea; pages 53-105, all clothing and accessories stills: Nathan Sayers, styled by Joseph La Corte and Ting Ting Lin; page 74: courtesy Mark Walsh and Leslie Chin; pages 106-107: Joseph La Corte; pages 136-137: "The Model," "Building the Set," "Before Shooting," and "The Wedding China": Jeremy Conway; Page 140: kitchen, blue vase, butterflies, and wine bottles: Jeremy Conway; pages 142-143: Jeremy Conway; page 145, top right: Jeremy Conway; page 148: Jeremy Conway; page 149, bottom right: Jeremy Conway; page 153, upper right: Eric Cyphers; page 154, photo of bed: Eric Cyphers; page 156, upper right and bottom: Jeremy Conway; page 157, upper right: Jeremy Conway; page 158: Eric Cyphers; page 161: top left and bottom: Melinda Relyea

MELCHER MEDIA

124 West 13th Street , New York, NY 10011
www.melcher.com

Publisher: Charles Melcher
Associate Publisher: Bonnie Eldon
Editor in Chief: Duncan Bock

Executive Editor and Project Manager: Lia Ronnen
Project Editor: Megan Worman
Production Director: Kurt Andrews
Production Assistant: Daniel del Valle
Contributing Editor: Melinda Relyea

DESIGNED BY
Number 17, NYC